HTML

THE BASICS OF DESIGNING WEBPAGES

For B.Sc(Computer Science)., B.C.A., M.Sc., M.C.A Courses

By

S. SYDHANI BEGUM

DESCRIPTION

HTML – The Basics of Designing Webpages book contains simple forms of creating webpage using the HTML language.

This book will help the beginners to easily learn how to create the webpages in an easy way, which is useful for the Beginners to learn.

I hope this book will be very useful to all the Beginners to learn about HTML to create attractive webpages.

I wish all the Beginners to learn very fast and in an effective manner.

And I wish to pray for the Success of this Book.

S. SYDHANI BEGUM

CONTENTS

HTML

HTML is the standard markup language for designing the Web pages.

- HTML stands for Hyper Text Markup Language
- HTML used to display the Web pages using markup tags
- HTML elements are the building blocks of HTML pages
- HTML elements are represented by tags
- HTML tags are surrounded by the two characters < and >
- The surrounding characters are called angle brackets
- HTML tags normally come in pairs like <b> and </b>
- HTML tags are in pairs as start tag and end tag
- HTML tags label pieces of content such as "heading", "paragraph", "table", and so on
- Browsers do not display the HTML tags, but use them to render the content of the page

HTML Tags

HTML tags are element names surrounded by angle brackets:
<tagname>content goes here...</tagname>

- HTML tags normally come **in pairs** like <p> and </p>

- The first tag in a pair is the **start tag,** the second tag is the **end tag**
- The end tag is written like the start tag, but with a **forward slash** inserted before the tag name
- The start tag is also called the opening tag, and the end tag the closing tag.

A Simple HTML Document

```
<!DOCTYPE html>
<html>
<head>
<title>Page Title</title>
</head>
<body>
<h1>My First Heading</h1>
<p>My first paragraph.</p>
</body>
</html>
```

Example Details

- The <!DOCTYPE html> declaration defines this document to be HTML5
- The <html> element is the root element of an HTML page
- The <head> element contains meta information about the document
- The <title> element specifies a title for the document

- The <body> element contains the visible page content
- The <h1> element defines a large heading
- The <p> element defines a paragraph

Web Browsers

The purpose of a web browser (Chrome, IE, Firefox, Safari) is to read HTML documents and display them.

The browser does not display the HTML tags, but uses them to determine how to display the document:

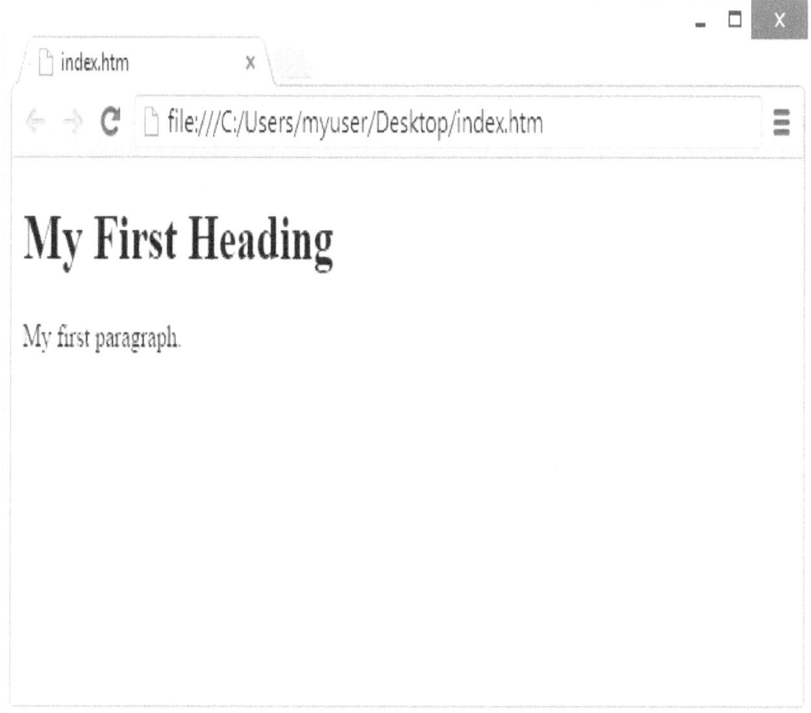

HTML Page Structure

Below is a visualization of an HTML page structure:

<html>

<head>

<title>Page title</title>

</head>

<body>

<h1>This is a heading</h1>

<p>This is a paragraph.</p>

<p>This is another paragraph.</p>

</body>

</html>

Note: Only the content inside the <body> section is displayed in a browser.

The <!DOCTYPE> Declaration

- The <!DOCTYPE> declaration represents the document type, and helps browsers to display web pages correctly.
- It must only appear once, at the top of the page (before any HTML tags).
- The <!DOCTYPE> declaration is not case sensitive.
- The <!DOCTYPE> declaration for HTML5 is:

<!DOCTYPE html>

HTML Versions

Since the early days of the web, there have been many versions of HTML:

Version	Year
HTML	1991
HTML 2.0	1995
HTML 3.2	1997
HTML 4.01	1999
XHTML	2000
HTML5	2014

HTML Editors

- Write HTML Using Notepad or any Text Editors
- Web pages can be created and modified by using professional HTML editors.
- However, for learning HTML a simple text editor like Notepad (PC) or Text Edit (Mac) are most commonly used.
- Follow the four steps below to create your first web page with **Notepad or Text Editor**.

Step 1: For Windows 8 or later

- Open Notepad (PC)
- Open the **Start Screen** (the window symbol at the bottom left on your screen).
- Type **Notepad**.

For Windows 7 or earlier

- Open **Start** > **Programs** > **Accessories** > **Notepad**

Step 2:

- Type or copy the HTML Program
- Write or copy some HTML into Notepad.

```
<!DOCTYPE html>
<html>
<body>
<h1>My First Heading</h1>
<p>My first paragraph.</p>
</body>
</html>
```

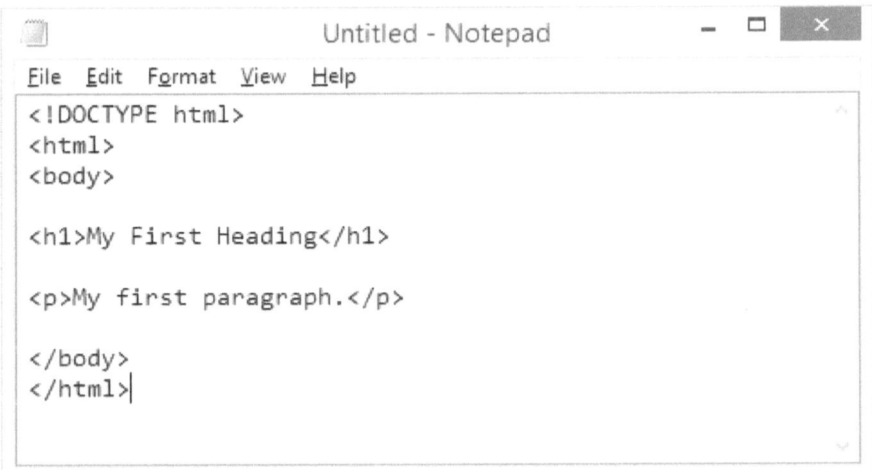

Step 3:

- Save the HTML Page

- Save the file on your computer. Select **File > Save as** in the Notepad menu.

- Name the file **"index.html"** or **"index.htm"** and set the encoding to **UTF-8** (which is the preferred encoding for HTML files).

- You can use either .htm or .html as file extension. There is no difference, it is up to you.

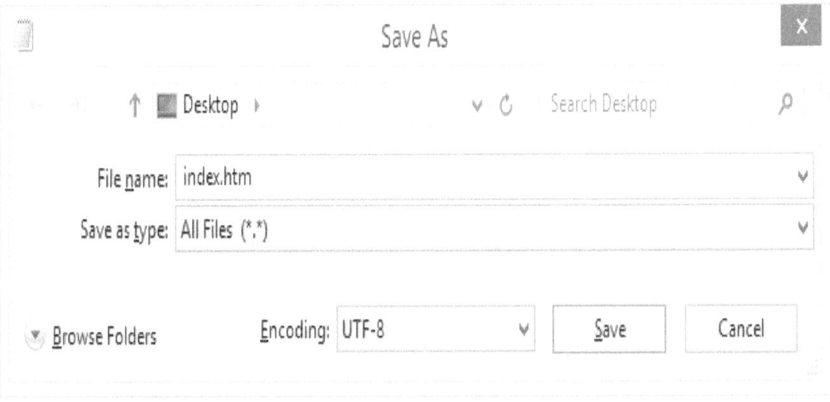

Step 4:

- View the HTML Page in Your Browser

- Open the saved HTML file in your favorite browser

- Double click on the file, or right-click - and choose "Open with" and click on the Web Browser name such as Google Chrome or Internet Explorer.

The result will look much like this:

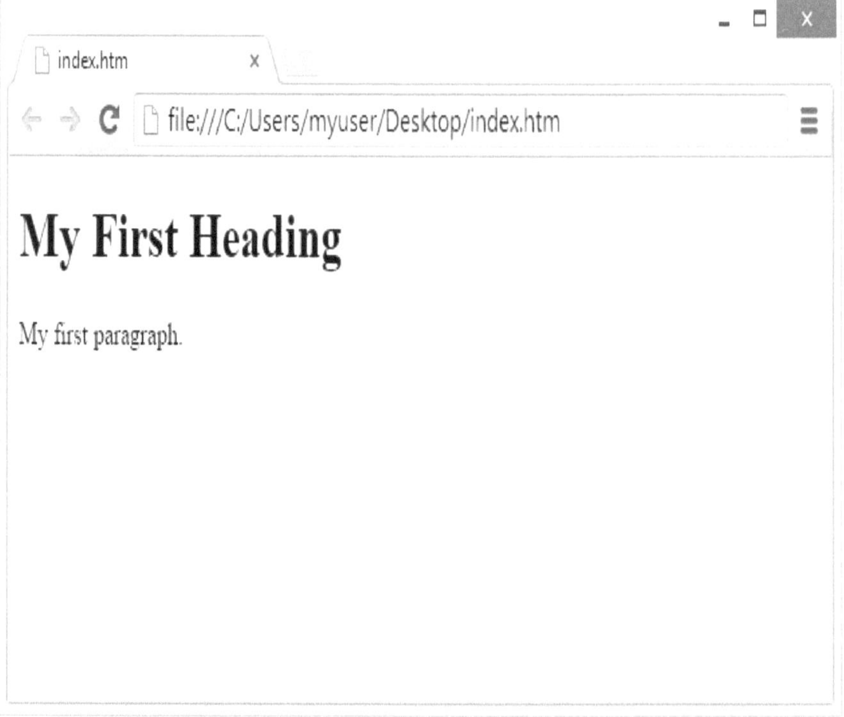

Online Editor

- With our free online editor, you can edit HTML code and view the result in your browser.

- It is the perfect tool when you want to **test** code fast.

- It also has color coding and the ability to save and share code with others:

Example

```
<!DOCTYPE html>
<html>
<head>
<title>Page Title</title>
</head>
<body>
<h1>This is a Heading</h1>
<p>This is a paragraph.</p>
</body>
</html>
```

HTML Elements

- An HTML element usually consists of a **start** tag and **end** tag, with the content inserted in between:

```
<tagname>Content goes here...</tagname>
```

- The HTML **element** is everything from the start tag to the end tag

```
<p>My first paragraph.</p>
```

<h1>Heading 1</h1>

- HTML elements with no content are called empty elements.
- Empty elements do not have an end tag, such as the <br> element (which indicates a line break).

Nested HTML Elements

- HTML elements can be nested (elements can contain elements).
- All HTML documents consist of nested HTML elements.
- This example contains four HTML elements:

Example

```
<!DOCTYPE html>
<html>
<body>
<h1>My First Heading</h1>
<p>My first paragraph.</p>
</body>
</html>
```

Example Explained

- The <html> element defines the **whole document**.
- It has a **start** tag <html> and an **end** tag </html>.
- The <body> element defines the **document body**.
- It has a **start** tag <body> and an **end** tag </body>.
- The element **content** is two other HTML elements (<h1> and <p>).

```
<body>
<h1>My First Heading</h1>
<p>My first paragraph.</p>
</body>
```

- The <h1> element defines a **heading**.
- It has a **start** tag <h1> and an **end** tag </h1>.
- The element **content** is: My First Heading.
- <h1>My First Heading</h1>
- The <p> element defines a **paragraph**.
- It has a **start** tag <p> and an **end** tag </p>.
- The element **content** is: My first paragraph.

```
<p>My first paragraph.</p>
```

Do Not Forget the End Tag

Some HTML elements will display correctly, even if you forget the end tag:

Example

```
<html>
<body>
<p>This is a paragraph
<p>This is a paragraph
</body>
</html>
```

The example above works in all browsers, because the closing tag is considered optional.

Never rely on this. It might produce unexpected results and/or errors if you forget the end tag.

Empty HTML Elements

- HTML elements with no content are called empty elements.
- The <br> is an empty element without a closing tag (the <br> tag defines a line break).
- Empty elements can be "closed" in the opening tag like this: <br />.
- HTML5 does not require empty elements to be closed. But if you want stricter validation, or if you need to make your document readable by XML parsers, you must close all HTML elements properly.

Use Lowercase Tags

- HTML tags are not case sensitive:

    <P> means the same as <p>.

- The HTML5 standard does not require lowercase tags, but W3C **recommends** lowercase in HTML, and **demands** lowercase for stricter document types like XHTML.
- Always use lowercase tags.
- Attributes provide additional information about HTML elements.

HTML Attributes

- All HTML elements can have **attributes**
- Attributes provide **additional information** about an element
- Attributes are always specified in **the start tag**
- Attributes usually come in name/value pairs like: **name="value"**

Here, a title attribute is added to the <p> element.

The value of the title attribute will be displayed as a tooltip when you mouse over the paragraph:

Example

```
<p title="I'm a tooltip">
This is a paragraph.
</p>
```

Single or Double Quotes?

- Double quotes around attribute values are the most common in HTML, but single quotes can also be used.
- In some situations, when the attribute value itself contains double quotes, it is necessary to use single quotes:

```
<p title='Sai "Nath" Shiv'>
```

Or vice versa:

```
<p title="Sai ' Nath' Shiv">
```

To View HTML Source

- Right-click in an HTML page and select "View Page Source" (in Chrome) or "View Source" (in IE), or similar in other browsers. This will open a window containing the HTML source code of the page.

- Inspect an HTML Element:

- Right-click on an element (or a blank area), and choose "Inspect" or "Inspect Element" to see what elements are made up of (you will see both the HTML and the CSS).

- You can also edit the HTML or CSS on-the-fly in the Elements or Styles panel that opens.

Basic HTML Tags

Tag	Description
<html>	Defines the root of an HTML document
<body>	Defines the document's body
<head>	A container for all the head elements (title, scripts, styles, meta information, and more)
<h1> to <h6>	Defines HTML headings
<hr>	Defines a thematic change in the content

The HTML <head> Element

- The <head> element is a container for metadata.

- HTML metadata is data about the HTML document. Metadata is not displayed.

- The <head> element is placed between the <html> tag and the <body> tag:

Example
<html>
<head>
 <title>My First HTML</title>
</head>
<body>

.

.

</body>
<html>

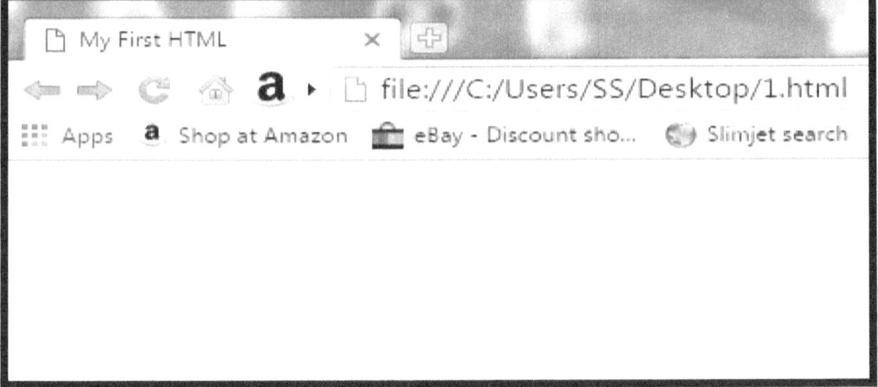

Meta data:

- HTML metadata is data about the HTML document. Metadata is not displayed.

- Metadata typically define the document title, character set, styles, links, scripts, and other meta information.

- The following tags describe metadata:

- <title>, <style>, <meta>, <link>, <script>, and <base>.

- Metadata is used by browsers (how to display content), by search engines (keywords), and other web services.

Define the character set used:

<meta charset="UTF-8">

Define a description of your web page:

<meta name="description" content="Free Web tutorials">

Define keywords for search engines:

<meta name="keywords" content="HTML, CSS, XML, JavaScript">

Define the author of a page:

<meta name="author" content="John Doe">

Refresh document every 30 seconds:

<meta http-equiv="refresh" content="30">

Example

<meta charset="UTF-8">

<meta name="description" content="Free Web tutorials">

<meta name="keywords" content="HTML,CSS,XML,JavaScript">

<meta name="author" content="John Doe">

HTML Comments

- Comment tags are used to insert comments in the HTML source code.

- You can add comments to your HTML source by using the following **syntax:**

    <!-- Write your comments here -->

- Notice that there is **an exclamation point (!) in the opening tag, but not in the closing tag.**

- Comments are not displayed by the browser, but they can help document your HTML source code.

- With comments you can place notifications and reminders in your HTML:

Example

<!-- This is a comment -->

<p>This is a paragraph.</p>

<!-- Add information for your comments -->

- Comments are also great for debugging HTML, because you can comment out HTML lines of code, one at a time, to search for errors:

Example

<!-- Do not display this at the moment

<img border="0" src="pic_trulli.jpg" alt="Trulli">

-->

HTML Headings

- Headings are defined with the <h1> to <h6> tags.

- <h1> defines the most important heading.

- <h6> defines the least important heading.

Example

<h1>Heading 1</h1>

<h2>Heading 2</h2>

<h3>Heading 3</h3>

<h4>Heading 4</h4>

<h5>Heading 5</h5>

<h6>Heading 6</h6>

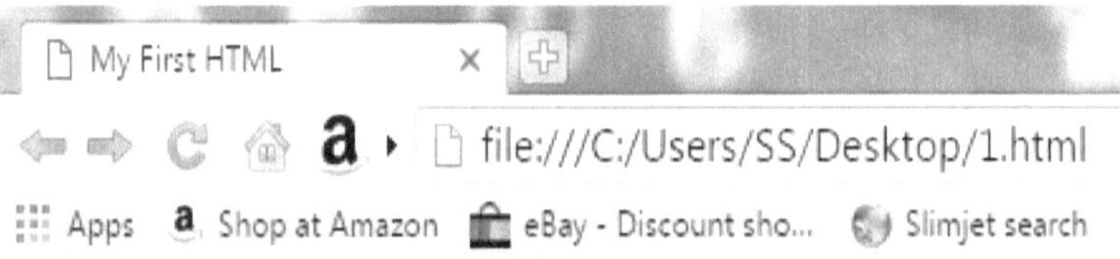

Heading 1

Heading 2

Heading 3

Heading 4

Heading 5

Heading 6

HTML Horizontal Rules

- The <hr> tag defines a thematic break in an HTML page, and is most often displayed as a horizontal rule.
- The <hr> element is used to separate content (or define a change) in an HTML page.

Example

```
<h1>This is heading 1</h1>
<p>This is some text.</p>
<hr>
<h2>This is heading 2</h2>
<p>This is some other text.</p>
<hr>
```

HTML Image

- HTML images are defined with the <img> tag.

- The filename of the image source is specified in the src attribute:

- The <img> tag is empty, it contains attributes only, and does not have a closing tag.

- The src attribute specifies the URL (web address) of the image:

<img src="url">

Example

<img src="img_flower.jpg">

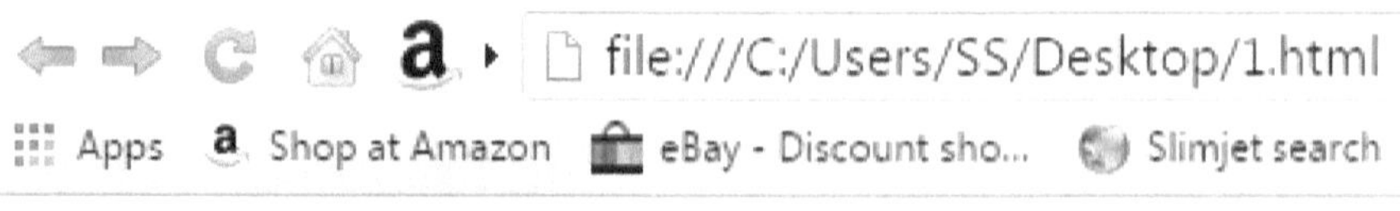

The width and height Attributes

- Images in HTML have a set of **size** attributes, which specifies the width and height of the image:

Example

```
<img src="img_flower.jpg" width="500" height="600">
```

- The image size is specified in pixels.
- width="500" means 500 pixels wide.

The alt Attribute

- The alt attribute specifies an alternative text to be used, when an image cannot be displayed.
- The value of the attribute can be read by screen readers.

Example

```
<img src="img_flower.jpg" alt="Flowers garden">
```

- The alt attribute is also useful if the image does not exist
  Images in Another Folder
- If not specified, the browser expects to find the image in the same folder as the web page.
- However, it is common to store images in a sub-folder.
- You must then include the folder name in the src attribute:

Example

```
<img src="/images/flowers.gif" alt="Flower Gif"
style="width:128px;height:128px;">
```

Images on Another Server

- Some web sites store their images on image servers.
- Actually, you can access images from any web address in the world.

Example

<img src="https://www.google.com/images/greengarden.jpg"
alt="garden image">

Image as a Link

- To use an image as a link, put the <img> tag inside the <a> tag.

Example

<a href="new.html">
  <img src="smiley.gif" alt="HTML image link">
</a>

HTML Links

- HTML links are hyperlinks.
- You can click on a link and jump to another document.
- When you move the mouse over a link, the mouse arrow will turn into a little hand.
- Links are found in nearly all web pages. Links allow users to click their way from page to page.
- A link does not have to be text. It can be an image or any other HTML element.

Syntax

- In HTML, links are defined with the <a> tag:

<a href="*url*">*link text*</a>

HTML Links – with href

- HTML links are defined with the <a> tag. The link address is specified in the href attribute:

Example

<a href="https://www.google.com">This is a link</a>

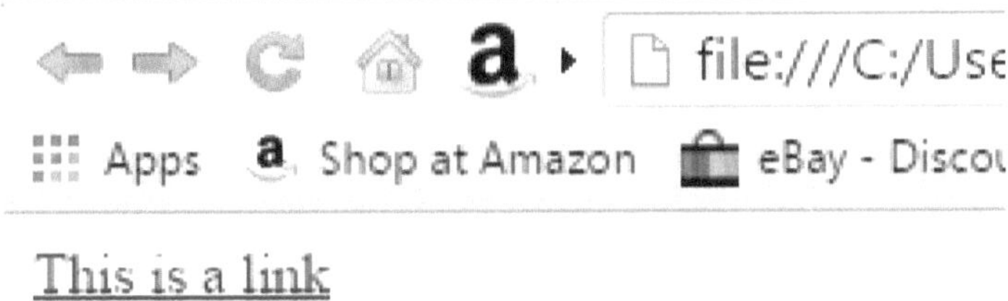

HTML Link Colors

By default, a link will appear in all browsers as an:

- An unvisited link is underlined and blue
- A visited link is underlined and purple
- An active link is underlined and red

You can change the default colors, by using CSS,

Example

```
<style>
a:link {
  color: green;
  background-color: transparent;
  text-decoration: none;
}
```

```
a:visited {
  color: pink;
  background-color: transparent;
  text-decoration: none;
}


a:hover {
  color: red;
  background-color: transparent;
  text-decoration: underline;
}


a:active {
  color: yellow;
  background-color: transparent;
  text-decoration: underline;
}
</style>
```

But the CSS files need to be saved with the .css extension.

HTML Links - The target attribute

The target attribute specifies where to open the linked document.

The target attribute can have one of the following values:

- _blank - Opens the linked document in a new window or tab

- _self - Opens the linked document in the same window/tab as it was clicked (this is default)
- _parent - Opens the linked document in the parent frame
- _top - Opens the linked document in the full body of the window
- FRAMENAME - Opens the linked document in a named frame

This example will open the linked document in a new browser window/tab:

<a href="https://www.google.com/" target="_blank">Visit Google</a>

 If your webpage is locked in a frame, you can use target="_top" to break out of the frame:

<a href="https://www.india.com/html/" target="_top">Target Attribute!</a>

Link Titles

- The title attribute specifies extra information about an element.
- The information is most often shown as a tooltip text when the mouse moves over the element.

Example

<a href="https://www.india.com/html/" title="Go to india HTML section">our country India</a>

HTML Text Formatting Elements

- HTML also defines special **elements** for defining text with a special **meaning**.
- HTML uses elements like <b> and <i> for formatting output, like **bold** or *italic* text.
- Formatting elements were designed to display special types of text:

  - > <b> - Bold text
  - > <i> - Italic text
  - > <u> - Underline text
  - > <em> - Emphasized text
  - > <mark> - Marked text
  - > <small> - Small text
  - > <big> - Big text
  - > <del> - Deleted text
  - > <ins> - Inserted text
  - > <sub> - Subscript text
  - > <sup> - Superscript text
  - > <strong> - Important text
  - > <tt> - Typewriter text
  - > <kbd> - Keyboard text

HTML <b> and <strong> Elements

The HTML <b> element defines **bold** text, without any extra importance.

Example

<b>This text is bold</b>

The HTML <strong> element defines **strong** text, with added semantic "strong" importance.

Example

<strong>This text is strong</strong>

Output:

This text is bold

HTML <i> and <em> Elements

The HTML <i> element defines ITALIC text, without any extra importance.

The HTML <em> element defines EMPHASIZED text, with added semantic importance.

Example

<i>This text is italic</i>

Output:

This text is italic

Example

<em>This text is emphasized</em>

Note : Browsers display **<strong> as <b>, and <em> as <i>.**

However, there is a difference in the meaning of these tags:

<b> and <i> defines bold and italic text,

But **<strong> and <em>** means that the **text is**

"important".

HTML <small> Element

The HTML <small> element defines smaller text.

Example

<h2>HTML <small>Small</small> Formatting</h2>

HTML <mark> Element

The HTML <mark> element defines marked or highlighted text.

Example

<h2>HTML <mark>Marked</mark> Formatting</h2>

HTML <del> Element

The HTML <del> element defines ~~deleted~~ (removed) text.

Example

<p>My favorite color is <del>blue</del> red.</p>

HTML <ins> Element

The HTML <ins> element defines inserted (added) text.

Example

<p>My favorite <ins>color</ins> is red.</p>

HTML <sub> Element

The HTML <sub> element defines subscripted text.

Example

<p>This is _{subscripted} text.</p>

HTML <sup> Element

The HTML <sup> element defines superscripted text.

Example

<p>This is ^{superscripted} text.</p>

Text Formatting Output in browser will be shown as:

Bold Text
Italic Text
<u>Underline Text</u>
Emphasized text
Marked Text
Small Text
Big Text
~~Deleted Text~~
<u>Inserted Text</u>
H_2O Subscript

4th Superscript
Important text
Typewriter text
Keyboard text

HTML Quotation and Citation Elements

Tag	Description
<abbr>	Defines an abbreviation or acronym
<address>	Defines contact information for the author/owner of a document
<bdo>	Defines the text direction
<blockquote>	Defines a section that is quoted from another source
<cite>	Defines the title of a work
<q>	Defines a short inline quotation

HTML <q> for Short Quotations

- The HTML <q> element defines a short quotation.
- Browsers usually insert quotation marks around the <q> element.

Example

<p>WWF's goal is to: <q>Build a future where people live in harmony with nature.</q></p>

HTML <abbr> for Abbreviations

- The HTML <abbr> element defines an abbreviation or an acronym.

- Marking abbreviations can give useful information to browsers, translation systems and search-engines.

Example

<p>The <abbr title="World Health Organization">WHO</abbr> was founded in 1948.</p>

HTML <address> for Contact Information

- The HTML <address> element defines contact information (author/owner) of a document or an article.
- The <address> element is usually displayed in italic.
- Most browsers will add a line break before and after the element.

Example

<address>

Written by John .

Visit us at:

Example.com

Box 786, Poonthamalli

Chennai

</address>

HTML <cite> for Work Title

- The HTML <cite> element defines the title of a work.
- Browsers usually display <cite> elements in italic.

Example

<p><cite>The Scream</cite> by Edvard Munch. Painted in 1893.</p>

HTML Tables

- An **HTML table** is defined with the **<table> tag**.
- The <table> tag has lots of **attributes** like sett ing the **table color, border, size of the table border etc**.
- Each **table row** is defined with the **<tr> tag – table row**.
- A **table header** is defined with the **<th> tag – table head**.
- A **table data/cell** is defined with the **<td> tag – table data**.
- The **<td> elements** are the data containers of the table. They can contain all sorts of HTML elements: text, images, lists, other tables, etc.

By default, table headings are bold and centered.

Example

```
<table color="blue" border="10">
 <tr>
  <th>Firstname</th>
  <th>Lastname</th>
  <th>Age</th>
 </tr>
 <tr>
  <td>Sai</td>
  <td>Nath</td>
  <td>50</td>
 </tr>
```

```
<tr>
  <td>Shiva</td>
  <td>Kumar</td>
  <td>94</td>
 </tr>
</table>
```

Firstname	Lastname	Age
Sai	Nath	50
Shiva	Kumar	94

Colspan - Cells that Span Many Columns

To make a cell span more than one column, use the colspan attribute.

Example

```
<table style="width:100%">
 <tr>
   <th>Name</th>
   <th colspan="2">Telephone</th>
 </tr>
 <tr>
   <td>Tim Bernees Lee</td>
   <td>55577854</td>
   <td>55577855</td>
 </tr>
</table>
```

Rowspan - Cells that Span Many Rows

To make a cell span more than one row, use the rowspan attribute.

Example

```
<table style="width:100%">
 <tr>
  <th>Name:</th>
  <td>Tim Bernees Lee</td>
 </tr>
 <tr>
  <th rowspan="2">Telephone:</th>
  <td>55577854</td>
 </tr>
 <tr>
  <td>55577855</td>
 </tr>
</table>
```

Adding a Caption

- To add a caption to a table, use the <caption> tag
- The <caption> tag must be inserted immediately after the <table> tag.

Example

```
<table>
 <caption>Monthly savings</caption>
 <tr>
  <th>Month</th>
  <th>Savings</th>
```

```
</tr>
<tr>
 <td>January</td>
 <td>$100</td>
</tr>
<tr>
 <td>February</td>
 <td>$50</td>
</tr>
</table>
```

Output:

Monthly savings

Month   Savings

January $100

February $50

HTML Table Tags

Tag	Description
<table>	Defines a table
<th>	Defines a header cell in a table
<tr>	Defines a row in a table
<td>	Defines a cell in a table
<caption>	Defines a table caption
<colgroup>	Specifies a group of one or more columns in a table for formatting
<col>	Specifies column properties for each column within a <colgroup> element
<thead>	Groups the header content in a table
<tbody>	Groups the body content in a table
<tfoot>	Groups the footer content in a table

HTML Lists

There are two types of HTML lists are available they are:

1. Unordered list
2. Ordered List

Unordered HTML List

- An unordered list starts with the <ul> tag.

- Each list item starts with the <li> tag.

- The list items will be marked with bullets (small black circles) by default,

Example

```
<ul>
 <li>Ice cream</li>
 <li>Tea</li>
 <li>Lemon juice</li>
</ul>
```

An Unordered List

- Ice cream
- Tea
- Lemon juice

Unordered HTML List attributes:

Value	Description
disc	Sets the list item marker to a bullet (default)
Circle	Sets the list item marker to a circle

square   Sets the list item marker to a square

None   The list items will not be marked

Example - Disc

```
<ul type="disc">
 <li>Ice cream</li>
  <li>Tea</li>
  <li>Lemon juice</li>
</ul>
```


Example - Circle

```
<ul type="circle">
 <li>Ice cream</li>
  <li>Tea</li>
  <li>Lemon juice</li>
</ul>
```


Example - Square

```
<ul type="square">
<li>Ice cream</li>
  <li>Tea</li>
  <li>Lemon juice</li>
</ul>
```

Example - None

```
<ul type="none">
 <li>Ice cream</li>
  <li>Tea</li>
  <li>Lemon juice</li>
</ul>
```

Output:

- Ice cream
- Tea
- Lemon juice

- Ice cream
- Tea
- Lemon juice

- Ice cream
- Tea
- Lemon juice

- Ice cream
- Tea
- Lemon juice

Ordered HTML List

- An ordered list starts with the <ol> tag. Each list item starts with the <li> tag.

- The list items will be marked with numbers by default:

Example

```
<ol>
<li>Ice cream</li>
 <li>Tea</li>
 <li>Lemon juice</li>
</ol>
```

An Ordered List:

1. Ice cream
2. Tea
3. Lemon jiuce

Ordered List - Type Attribute

The type attribute of the <ol> tag, defines the type of the list item marker:

Type	Description
type="1"	The list items will be numbered with numbers (default)
type="A"	The list items will be numbered with uppercase letters
type="a"	The list items will be numbered with lowercase

	letters
type="I"	The list items will be numbered with uppercase roman numbers
type="i"	The list items will be numbered with lowercase roman numbers

Numbers:

```
<ol type="1">
<li>Ice cream</li>
  <li>Tea</li>
  <li>Lemon juice</li>
</ol>
```

Uppercase Letters:

```
<ol type="A">
<li>Ice cream</li>
  <li>Tea</li>
  <li>Lemon juice</li>
</ol>
```

Lowercase Letters:

```
<ol type="a">
 <li>Ice cream</li>
  <li>Tea</li>
  <li>Lemon juice</li>
</ol>
```

Uppercase Roman Numbers:

```
<ol type="I">
<li>Ice cream</li>
  <li>Tea</li>
  <li>Lemon juice</li>
</ol>
```

Lowercase Roman Numbers:

```
<ol type="i">
 <li>Ice cream</li>
  <li>Tea</li>
  <li>Lemon juice</li>
</ol>
```

Output:

```
    1.   Ice cream
    2.   Tea
    3.   Lemon juice

    A.   Ice cream
    B.   Tea
    C.   Lemon juice

    a.   Ice cream
    b.   Tea
    c.   Lemon juice

    I.   Ice cream
   II.   Tea
  III.   Lemon juice

    i.   Ice cream
   ii.   Tea
  iii.   Lemon juice
```

HTML Description Lists

- HTML also supports description lists.

- A description list is a list of terms, with a description of each term.

- The <dl> tag defines the description list, the <dt> tag defines the term (name), and the <dd> tag describes each term.

Example

```
<dl>
 <dt>Coffee</dt>
 <dd>- black hot drink</dd>
 <dt>Milk</dt>
 <dd>- white cold drink</dd>
</dl>
```

Output:

1. Ice cream
2. Tea
3. Lemon juice

Coffee
    - black hot drink
Milk
    - white cold drink

Nested HTML Lists

One List can be nested within the other list is called as the Nested HTML list(lists inside lists).

Example

```
<ul>
  <li>Ice cream</li>
  <li>Tea
    <ul>
      <li>Vanilla</li>
      <li>Chocolate</li>
    </ul>
  </li>
  <li>Juices</li>
</ul>
```

List items can contain new list, and other HTML elements, like images and links, etc.

Output:

- Ice cream
- Tea
    - Vanilla
    - Chocolate
- Juices

HTML Block and Inline Elements

- Every HTML element has a default display value depending on what type of element it is.
- The default display value for most elements is block or inline.

Block-level Elements

- A block-level element always starts on a new line and takes up the full width available.
- The <div> element is a block-level element.

Example
<div>Hello</div>
<div>World</div>

Block level elements in HTML are:

<address>, <article>, <aside>, <blockquote>, <canvas>, <dd>, <div>, <dl>, <dt>, <fieldset>, <figcaption>, <figure>, <footer>, <form>, <h1>-<h6>, <header>, <hr>, <li>, <main>, <nav>, <noscript>, <ol>, <output>, <p>, <pre>, <section>, <table>, <tfoot>, <ul>, <video>

Inline Elements

- An inline element does not start on a new line and only takes up as much width as necessary.
- This is an inline <span> element inside a paragraph.

Example

<span>Hello</span>

<span>World</span>

Inline elements in HTML:

<a>, <abbr>, <acronym>, <b>, <bdo>, <big>, <br>, <button>, <cite>, <code>,<dfn>, <em>, <i>, <img>, <input>, <kbd>, <label>, <map>, <object>, <q>, <samp>, <script>, <select>, <small>, <span>, <strong>, <sub>, <sup>, <textarea>, <time>, <tt>, <var>

The <div> Element

It defines a section in a document as block-level

- The <div> element is often used as a container for other HTML elements.
- The <div> element has no required attributes, but style, class and id are common.
- When used together with CSS, the <div> element can be used to style blocks of content:

Example

<div style="background-color:black; ">

 <h2>India</h2>

</div>

The <span> Element

- It defines a section in a document as inline.
- The <span> element is often used as a container for some text.

- The <span> element has no required attributes, but style, class and id are common.

- When used together with CSS, the <span> element can be used to style parts of the text:

Example

<h1>My <span style="color:red">Important</span> Heading</h1>

HTML Forms

The <form> Element

- The HTML <form> element defines a form that is used to collect user input through various HTML form elements.

- An HTML form contains several **form elements**.

- Form elements are different types of input elements, like text fields, checkboxes, radio buttons, submit buttons, and more.

Syntax:

<form>

.

form elements

.

</form>

HTML Form Elements

Tag	Description
<form>	Defines an HTML form for user input
<input>	Defines an input control
<textarea>	Defines a multiline input control (text area)
<label>	Defines a label for an <input> element
<fieldset>	Groups related elements in a form
<legend>	Defines a caption for a <fieldset> element
<select>	Defines a drop-down list
<optgroup>	Defines a group of related options in a drop-down list
<option>	Defines an option in a drop-down list
<button>	Defines a clickable button
<datalist>	Specifies a list of pre-defined options for input controls
<output>	Defines the result of a calculation

The <input> Element

- The most important form element is the <input> element.

- The <input> element can be displayed in several ways, depending on the type attribute.

Example

<input name="firstname" type="text">

- If the type attribute is omitted, the input field gets the default type: "text".

- The <input> element is the most important form element.

- The <input> element can be displayed in several ways, depending on the **type** attribute.

Here are some examples:

Type	Description
<input type="text">	Defines a one-line text input field
<input type="radio">	Defines a radio button (for selecting one of many choices)
<input type="submit">	Defines a submit button (for submitting the form)

Text Input

- <input type="text"> defines a one-line input field for **text input**.

- The form itself is not visible. Also note that the default width of a text field is 20 characters.

Example

```
<form>
  First name:<br>
  <input type="text" name="firstname"><br>
  Last name:<br>
  <input type="text" name="lastname">
</form>
```

It will look like in a browser:

First name:

Last name:

Radio Button Input

Radio buttons allow a user select ONE of a limited number of choices.

Syntax:

<input type="radio"> defines a **radio button**.

Example

```
<form>
  <input type="radio" name="gender" value="male" checked> Male<br>
  <input type="radio" name="gender" value="female"> Female<br>
  <input type="radio" name="gender" value="other"> Other
</form>
```

It will be displayed in a browser as:

- Male

- Female

- Other

Password Input Type

The Password Input type allow the user to enter the values in a password form such as invisible text.

Syntax:

<input type="password"> defines a **password field**:

Example

<form>

  User name:

  <input type="text" name="username">

  User password:

  <input type="password" name="psw">

</form>

It will be displayed in a browser:

User name:

SAI

User password:

***

The characters in a password field are masked (shown as asterisks or circles).

Reset Input Type

The Reset type is used to reset the form which means the form will delete the entered values in the form and shows an empty form.

Syntax:

<input type="reset"> defines a **reset button**

That will reset all form values to their default values:

Example

```
<form action="/action_page.php">
  First name:<br>
  <input type="text" name="firstname" value="Sai"><br>
  Last name:<br>
  <input type="text" name="lastname" value="Samar"><br><br>
  <input type="submit" value="Submit">
  <input type="reset">
</form>
```

It will be displayed in a browser as:

First name:

Sai

Last name:

Samar

Submit   Reset

If you change the input values and then click the "Reset" button, the form-data will be reset to the default values.

Checkbox Input Type

Checkboxes let a user select ZERO or MORE options of a limited number of choices.

Syntax:

<input type="checkbox"> defines a **checkbox**.

Example

```
<form>
  <input type="checkbox" name="vehicle1" value="Bike"> I have a
bike<br>
  <input type="checkbox" name="vehicle2" value="Car"> I have a
car
</form>
```

It will be displayed in a browser as:

☐   I have a cycle

☑   I have a car

Button Input Type

The Button input type allow the user to perform an action when they click on the Button.

Syntax:

<input type="button"> defines a clickable **button.**

Example

```
<input type="button" onclick="alert('Hello World!')" value="Click
Me!">
```

The Submit Button

- The server page will process the data when the user used to submit the value from the form to the form handler.

- This is done using the Submit input type.

Syntax:

<input type="submit"> defines a button for **submitting** the form data to a **form-handler**.

The form-handler is specified in the form's **action** attribute.

Example

```
<form action="action.php">
 First name:<br>
 <input type="text" name="firstname" value="Sai"><br>
 Last name:<br>
 <input type="text" name="lastname" value="Smar"><br><br>
 <input type="submit" value="Submit">
</form>
```

It will be displayed in a browser as:

First name:

Sai

Last name:

Samar

Submit

HTML Input Attributes

The value Attribute

The value attribute specifies the initial value for an input field.

Example

```
<form action="">
  First name:<br>
  <input type="text" name="firstname" value="John">
</form>
```

The read only Attribute

The readonly attribute specifies that the input field is read only

Example

```
<form action="">
  First name:<br>
  <input type="text" name="firstname" value="John" readonly>
</form>
```

The disabled Attribute

- The disabled attribute specifies that the input field is disabled.

- A disabled input field is unusable and un-clickable, and its value will not be sent when submitting the form.

Example

```
<form action="">
  First name:<br>
  <input type="text" name="firstname" value="John" disabled>
</form>
```

The size Attribute

The size attribute specifies the size (in characters) for the input field.

Example

```
<form action="">
 First name:<br>
 <input type="text" name="firstname" value="Jack" size="40">
</form>
```

The maxlength Attribute

The maxlength attribute specifies the maximum allowed length for the input field.

Example

```
<form action="">
 First name:<br>
 <input type="text" name="firstname" maxlength="10">
</form>
```

- With a maxlength attribute, the input field will not accept more than the allowed number of characters.
- The maxlength attribute does not provide any feedback. If you want to alert the user, you must write JavaScript code.

The Action Attribute

- The action attribute defines the action to be performed when the form is submitted.
- Normally, the form data is sent to a web page on the server when the user clicks on the submit button.

- The form data is sent to a page on the server called "action.php".

- This page contains a server-side script that handles the form data:

<form action="action.php">

- If the action attribute is omitted, the action is set to the current page.

The Target Attribute

- The target attribute specifies if the submitted result will open in a new browser tab, a frame, or in the current window.

- The default value is "_self" which means the form will be submitted in the current window.

- To make the form result open in a new browser tab, use the value "_blank":

Example

<form action="action.php" target="_blank">

The Name Attribute

- Each input field must have a name attribute to be submitted.

- If the name attribute is omitted, the data of that input field will not be sent at all.

Example

```
<form action="action.php">
  First name:<br>
  <input type="text" value="Mickey"><br>
  Last name:<br>
  <input type="text" name="lastname" value="Mouse"><br><br>
  <input type="submit" value="Submit">
</form>
```

The Method Attribute

- The method attribute specifies the HTTP method
  (**GET** or **POST**) to be used when submitting the form data.

Example

```
<form action="action.php" method="get">
```

or

```
<form action="action.php" method="post">
```

GET method

- The default method when submitting form data is GET.
- However, when GET is used, the submitted form data will
  be **visible in the page address** field as follows
  action.php?firstname=Mickey&lastname=Mouse
- The GET will Appends form-data into the URL in
  name/value pairs
- The length of a URL is limited (about 3000 characters)

- Never use GET to send sensitive data! (it will be visible in the URL)
- Useful for form submissions where a user wants to bookmark the result
- GET is better for non-secure data, like query strings in Google

POST method

- Always use POST if the form data contains sensitive or personal information.
- The POST method does not display the submitted form data in the page address field.
- POST has no size limitations, and can be used to send large amounts of data.
- Form submissions with POST cannot be bookmarked

Grouping Form Data with <fieldset>

- The <fieldset> element is used to group related data in a form.
- The <legend> element defines a caption for the <fieldset> element.

Example

```
<form action="/action_page.php">
 <fieldset>
  <legend>Personal information:</legend>
```

```
   First name:<br>
   <input type="text" name="firstname" value="Sai"><br>
   Last name:<br>
   <input type="text" name="lastname" value="Samar"><br><br>
   <input type="submit" value="Submit">
 </fieldset>
</form>
```

It will be displayed in a browser as:

Personal information:First name:

Sai

Last name:

Samar

Submit

List of all <form> attributes:

Attribute	Description
accept-charset	Specifies the charset used in the submitted form (default: the page charset).
action	Specifies an address (url) where to submit the form (default: the submitting page).
autocomplete	Specifies if the browser should autocomplete the form (default: on).
enctype	Specifies the encoding of the submitted data (default: is url-encoded).
method	Specifies the HTTP method used when submitting the form (default: GET).
name	Specifies a name used to identify the form (for DOM usage: document.forms.name).
novalidate	Specifies that the browser should not validate the form.
target	Specifies the target of the address in the action attribute (default: _self).

The <select> Element

- The <select> element defines a **drop-down list**

- The <option> elements defines an option that can be selected.
- By default, the first item in the drop-down list is selected.
- To define a pre-selected option, add the selected attribute to the option.

Example

```
<select name="Juices">
 <option value="pepsi">pepsi</option>
 <option value="Coca-cola">Coca-cola</option>
 <option value="Sprite">Sprite</option>
 <option value="Miranda">Miranda</option>
</select>
```

Example

```
<option value="sprite" selected>Sprite</option>
```

Visible Values:

Use the size attribute to specify the number of visible values.

Example

```
<select name="Juices" size="3">
 <option value="pepsi">pepsi</option>
 <option value="Coca-cola">Coca-cola</option>
 <option value="Sprite">Sprite</option>
 <option value="Miranda">Miranda</option>
</select>
```

Allow Multiple Selections:

Use the multiple attribute to allow the user to select more than one value:

Example

```
<select name="Juices" size="4" multiple>
  <option value="pepsi">pepsi</option>
  <option value="Coca-cola">Coca-cola</option>
  <option value="Sprite">Sprite</option>
  <option value="Miranda">Miranda</option>
</select>
```

The <textarea> Element

The <textarea> element defines a multi-line input field .

Example

```
<textarea name="message" rows="10" cols="30">
There was a beautiful flowers.
</textarea>
```

- The rows attribute specifies the visible number of lines in a text area.
- The cols attribute specifies the visible width of a text area.
- You can also define the size of the text area by using CSS.

Example

```
<textarea name="message" style="width:200px; height:600px">
There was a beautiful flowers.
</textarea>
```

Example Programs

A Program to illustrate text Font tag

```
<html>
<title> Font tag Example </title>
<body>
<font face="arial" size="1" color="blue"> WELCOME </font> <br>
<font size="2" color="cyan"> WELCOME </font> <br>
<font size="3" color="red"> WELCOME </font> <br>
<font size="4" color="yellow"> WELCOME </font> <br>
<font size="5" color="green"> WELCOME </font> <br>
<font size="6" color="brown"> WELCOME </font> <br>
<font size="7" color="pink"> WELCOME </font> <br>
<font size="20" color="gray"> WELCOME </font> <br>
</body>
</html>
```

A Program to illustrate comment,h1….h6, and div tag

```
<html>
<head>
<title> Illustrating comment, h1...h6 and div tags </title>
</head>
<body>
<!-- THIS IS A COMMENT LINE -->
<div style="color:#00ff00">
<h1 align="center"> This is h1 tag text with center aligned </h1>
<h2 align="left"> This is h2 tag text with left aligned </h2>
<h3 align="right">This is h3 tag text with right aligned </h3>
</div>
<h4> This is h4 tag text without alignment</h4>
<h5> This is h5 tag Text without alignment </h5>
<h6> This is h6 tag text without alignment </h6>
</body>
</html>
```

Illustrating comment, h1...h6 and div tags

This is h1 tag text with center aligned

This is h2 tag text with left aligned

This is h3 tag text with right aligned

This is h4 tag text without alignment

This is h5 tag Text without alignment

This is h6 tag text without alignment

A Program to illustrate text formatting tags

```
<html>
<head>
<title> Text Tags </title>
</head>
<body>
<center>
<h1 align="center">To illustrate text formatting tags </h1>
<hr color="red">
<P> <marquee behavior="alternate"> This is an alternate Marquee text
</marquee>
<p> This is <i> italized </i> </p>
<p> This is <u> underlined </u> </p>
<p> This is <b> bold </b> </p>
<p> This is <em> emphasized </em> </p>
<p>This is <Strong> Strong Text </strong> </p>
<p> This is <s> striked text </s> </p>
<p> This is <code> computer code </code> </p>
<p> This is <sup> superscript </sup> code </p>
<p> This is <sub> subscript </sub> code </p>
<p> This is <big> big text </big> </p>
<p> This is <small> small text </small> </p>
</center>
</body>

</html>
```

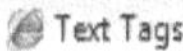

To illustrate text formatting tags

This is an alternate Marquee text

This is *italized*

This is <u>underlined</u>

This is **bold**

This is *emphasized*

This is **Strong Text**

This is ~~striked text~~

This is computer code

This is ^{superscript}code

This is $_{subscript}$code

This is big text

This is small text

A Program to illustrate the Ordered list

```
<html>
<head>
<title> Order List tag </title>
</head>
<body>
<ul type="disc">

 <li>Ice cream</li>

  <li>Tea</li>

  <li>Lemon juice</li>

</ul>
```

```
<ul type="circle">
 <li>Ice cream</li>
  <li>Tea</li>
  <li>Lemon juice</li>
</ul>

<ul type="square">
<li>Ice cream</li>
  <li>Tea</li>
  <li>Lemon juice</li>
</ul>
<ul type="none">
 <li>Ice cream</li>
  <li>Tea</li>
  <li>Lemon juice</li>
</ul>
</body>
</html>
```

- Ice cream
- Tea
- Lemon juice

- Ice cream
- Tea
- Lemon juice

- Ice cream
- Tea
- Lemon juice

- Ice cream
- Tea
- Lemon juice

A Program to illustrate Unordered List

```
<html>
<head>
<title> UnOrder List tag </title>
</head>
<body>
```

```html
<ol type="1">
<li>Ice cream</li>
  <li>Tea</li>
  <li>Lemon juice</li>
</ol>
<ol type="A">
<li>Ice cream</li>
  <li>Tea</li>
  <li>Lemon juice</li>
</ol>
<ol type="a">
 <li>Ice cream</li>
  <li>Tea</li>
  <li>Lemon juice</li>
</ol>
<ol type="I">
<li>Ice cream</li>
  <li>Tea</li>
  <li>Lemon juice</li>
</ol>
<ol type="i">
 <li>Ice cream</li>
  <li>Tea</li>
  <li>Lemon juice</li>
</ol>
</body>
</html>
```

1.   Ice cream
2.   Tea
3.   Lemon juice

A.   Ice cream
B.   Tea
C.   Lemon juice

a.   Ice cream
b.   Tea
c.   Lemon juice

I.   Ice cream
II.   Tea
III.   Lemon juice

i.   Ice cream
ii.   Tea
iii.   Lemon juice

A Program to illustrate Img tag

```
<html>
<head>
<title> Image Tag </title>
</head>
<body>
<h3 align="center" style="color:red"> To illustrate image tags</h3>
<hr>
<p>
<img src="flower.bmp" align="right" height="100" width="100"/>
This image is right aligned with the text
</p>
<br><br><br><br><hr>
<p>
<img src="flower.bmp" align="left" height="100" width="100"/>
This image is left aligned with the text
```

```
</p>
<br><br><br><br><hr>
This image is center aligned with the text.
<img src="flower.bmp" align="middle" height="100"
width="100"/>
<br><br><br><br><hr>
This image is bottom aligned with the text.
<img src="flower.bmp" align="bottom" height="100"
width="100"/>
<br><br><br><br><hr>
This image is top aligned with the text.
<img src="flower.bmp" align="top" height="100" width="100"/>
</body>
</html>
```

Image Tag

To illustrate image tags

This image is right aligned with the text

This image is left aligned with the text

This image is center aligned with the text.

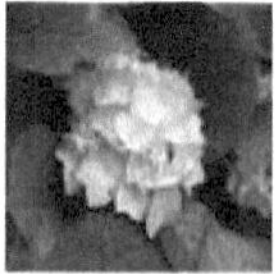
This image is bottom aligned with the text.

This image is top aligned with the text.

A Program to illustrate Hyper Link tag (Anchor tag)

Home.html

```
<html>
<head>
<title> Link Tag </title>
</head>
<title>
<body>
<h3 align="center" style="color:rcd">To illustrate link Tags</h3>
<hr>
Text as a link/hyperlink to another page : <a href="page1.html ">
Click here!!!</a>
<hr>
Image as a link/hyperlink :<a href="page1.html">
<img src="flower.bmp" width="32" height="32"
align="bottom"/></a>
<hr>
<p>
<a href="#C8">See also Chapter 8 ( link within a page )</a>
</p>
<h2>Chapter 1</h2>
<p>This chapter explains Pointers</p>
<h2>Chapter 2</h2>
<p>This chapter explains variables</p>
<h2>Chapter 3</h2>
<p>This chapter explains operator</p>
<h2>Chapter 4</a></h2>
<p>This chapter explains structure</p>
<h2>Chapter 5</h2>
<p>This chapter explains arrays</p>
<h2>Chapter 6</h2>
<p>This chapter explains linked list</p>
<h2>Chapter 7</h2>
<p>This chapter explains expressions</p>
<h2><a name="C8">Chapter 8</h2>
<p>This chapter explains Binary Trees</p>
<h2>Chapter 9</h2>
<p>This chapter explains Unordered trees</p>
```

```
<h2>Chapter 10</h2>
<p>This chapter explains Statements</p>
<h2>Chapter 11</h2>
<p>This chapter explains searching</p>
<h2>Chapter 12</h2><p>This chapter explains sorting</p>
<h2>Chapter 13</h2>
<p>This chapter explains Binary sort</p>
<h2>Chapter 14</h2>
<p>This chapter explains merge sort</p>
<h2>Chapter 15</h2>
<p>This chapter explains heap sort</p>
</body>
</html>
```

Page1.html
```
<html>
<head>
<title> Page1.html </title>
</head>
<body>
<h1 align="center"> Hello!!! This is a new chapter </h1>
<a href="home.html"> Go to home </a>
</body>
</html>
```

 Link Tag

To illustrate link Tags

Text as a link/hyperlink to another page : Click here!!!

Image as a link/hyperlink : 

See also Chapter 8 (link within a page)

Chapter 1

This chapter explains Pointers

Chapter 2

This chapter explains variables

Chapter 3

This chapter explains operator

Chapter 4

This chapter explains structure

Chapter 5

This chapter explains arrays

After Clicking On Click Me or the Flower image the output is

Hello!!! This is a new chapter

Go to home

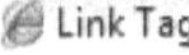

This chapter explains expressions

Chapter 8

This chapter explains Binary Trees

Chapter 9

This chapter explains Unordered trees

Chapter 10

This chapter explains Statements

Chapter 11

This chapter explains searching

Chapter 12

This chapter explains sorting

Chapter 13

This chapter explains Binary sort

Chapter 14

This chapter explains merge sort

Chapter 15

A Program to illustrate Form tag

```
<html>
<head>
<title> form tag </title>
</head>
<body>
<center>
<h3 align="center">To illustrate form based tags</h3> <hr
color="red">
<form action="">
<p>This is a text box to enter any text.<input type="text" >
<p>This is a text box to enter password.<input type="password" >
<p>This is a text area to enter large text<textarea> </textarea>
<p>This is a button.<input type="button" Value="Click" >
<p><b><u>Radio Options</u></b><br>
<input type="radio" name="y" checked> yes
<input type="radio" name="n" checked> no </p>
<p><b><u>Checkbox Options</u></b><br>
Sunday<input type="checkbox" checked >
Monday<input type="checkbox" >
Tuesday<input type="checkbox" >
</p>
<p><b><u>Menu driven options </u></b>
<select name="cars">
<option value="volvo">Volvo</option>
<option value="saab">Saab</option>
<option value="fiat">Fiat</option>
<option value="audi">Audi</option>
</select></p>
</form>
</center>
</body>
</html>
```

form tag

To illustrate form based tags

This is a text box to enter any text.

This is a text box to enter password.

This is a text area to enter large text

This is a button. Click

Radio Options
YES   NO

Checkbox Options
Sunday Monday Tuesday

Menu driven options Volvo

Volvo
Saab
Fiat
Audi

www.ingramcontent.com/pod-product-compliance
Lightning Source LLC
Chambersburg PA
CBHW031215160726
47992CB00006B/2743